Praxis French Sample Test

0173

Teacher Certification Exam

Teacher Certification Exam

By: Sharon Wynne, M.S.

"And, while there's no reason yet to panic, I think it's only prudent that we make preparations to panic."

XAMonline, INC.

Boston

To obtain permission(s) to use the material from this work for any purpose including workshops or seminars, please submit a written request to:

XAMonline, Inc.
25 First Street, Suite 106
Cambridge, MA 02141
Toll Free 1-800-509-4128
Email: info@xamonline.com
Web www.xamonline.com
Fax: 1-617-583-5552

Library of Congress Cataloging-in-Publication Data

Wynne, Sharon A.
French Sample Test 0173: Teacher Certification / Sharon A. Wynne. -2nd ed.
ISBN 978-1-60787-053-1
    1. French Sample Test 0173.   2. Study Guides.   3.
Praxis   4. Teachers' Certification & Licensure.   5. Careers

Disclaimer:
The opinions expressed in this publication are the sole works of XAMonline and were created independently from the National Education Association, Educational Testing Service, or any State Department of Education, National Evaluation Systems or other testing affiliates.

Between the time of publication and printing, state specific standards as well as testing formats and website information may change that is not included in part or in whole within this product. Sample test questions are developed by XAMonline and reflect similar content as on real tests; however, they are not former tests. XAMonline assembles content that aligns with state standards but makes no claims nor guarantees teacher candidates a passing score. Numerical scores are determined by testing companies such as NES or ETS and then are compared with individual state standards. A passing score varies from state to state.

Printed in the United States of America

PRAXIS: French Sample Test 0173
ISBN: 978-1-60787-053-1

TEACHER CERTIFICATION EXAM

TABLE OF CONTENTS

PG #

Great Study and Testing Tips!

What to study in order to prepare for the subject assessments is the focus of this study guide but equally important is *how* you study.

You can increase your chances of truly mastering the information by taking some simple, but effective steps.

Study Tips:

1. <u>Some foods aid the learning process</u>. Foods such as milk, nuts, seeds, rice, and oats help your study efforts by releasing natural memory enhancers called CCKs (*cholecystokinin*) composed of *tryptophan*, *choline*, and *phenylalanine*. All of these chemicals enhance the neurotransmitters associated with memory. Before studying, try a light, protein-rich meal of eggs, turkey, and fish. All of these foods release the memory enhancing chemicals. The better the connections, the more you comprehend.

Likewise, before you take a test, stick to a light snack of energy boosting and relaxing foods. A glass of milk, a piece of fruit, or some peanuts all release various memory-boosting chemicals and help you to relax and focus on the subject at hand.

2. <u>Learn to take great notes</u>. A by-product of our modern culture is that we have grown accustomed to getting our information in short doses (i.e. TV news sound bites or USA Today style newspaper articles.)

Consequently, we've subconsciously trained ourselves to assimilate information better in <u>neat little packages</u>. If your notes are scrawled all over the paper, it fragments the flow of the information. Strive for clarity. Newspapers use a standard format to achieve clarity. Your notes can be much clearer through use of proper formatting. A very effective format is called the <u>*"Cornell Method."*</u>

Take a sheet of loose-leaf lined notebook paper and draw a line all the way down the paper about 1-2" from the left-hand edge.

Draw another line across the width of the paper about 1-2" up from the bottom. Repeat this process on the reverse side of the page.

Look at the highly effective result. You have ample room for notes, a left hand margin for special emphasis items or inserting supplementary data from the textbook, a large area at the bottom for a brief summary, and a little rectangular space for just about anything you want.

3. <u>Get the concept then the details.</u> Too often we focus on the details and don't gather an understanding of the concept. However, if you simply memorize only dates, places, or names, you may well miss the whole point of the subject.

A key way to understand things is to put them in your own words. If you are working from a textbook, automatically summarize each paragraph in your mind. If you are outlining text, don't simply copy the author's words.

Rephrase them in your own words. You remember your own thoughts and words much better than someone else's, and subconsciously tend to associate the important details to the core concepts.

4. <u>Ask Why?</u> Pull apart written material paragraph by paragraph and don't forget the captions under the illustrations.

Example: If the heading is "Stream Erosion", flip it around to read "Why do streams erode?" Then answer the questions.

If you train your mind to think in a series of questions and answers, not only will you learn more, but it also helps to lessen the test anxiety because you are used to answering questions.

5. <u>Read for reinforcement and future needs.</u> Even if you only have 10 minutes, put your notes or a book in your hand. Your mind is similar to a computer; you have to input data in order to have it processed. *By reading, you are creating the neural connections for future retrieval.* The more times you read something, the more you reinforce the learning of ideas.

Even if you don't fully understand something on the first pass, *your mind stores much of the material for later recall.*

6. <u>Relax to learn so go into exile.</u> Our bodies respond to an inner clock called biorhythms. Burning the midnight oil works well for some people, but not everyone.

If possible, set aside a particular place to study that is free of distractions. Shut off the television, cell phone, pager and exile your friends and family during your study period.

If you really are bothered by silence, try background music. Light classical music at a low volume has been shown to aid in concentration over other types. Music that evokes pleasant emotions without lyrics are highly suggested. Try just about anything by Mozart. It relaxes you.

7. <u>Use arrows not highlighters</u>. At best, it's difficult to read a page full of yellow, pink, blue, and green streaks. Try staring at a neon sign for a while and you'll soon see that the horde of colors obscure the message.

A quick note, a brief dash of color, an underline, and an arrow pointing to a particular passage is much clearer than a horde of highlighted words.

8. <u>Budget your study time</u>. Although you shouldn't ignore any of the material, *allocate your available study time in the same ratio that topics may appear on the test.*

Testing Tips:

1. Get smart, play dumb. Don't read anything into the question. Don't make an assumption that the test writer is looking for something else than what is asked. Stick to the question as written and don't read extra things into it.

2. Read the question and all the choices *twice* before answering the question. You may miss something by not carefully reading, and then re-reading both the question and the answers.

If you really don't have a clue as to the right answer, leave it blank on the first time through. Go on to the other questions, as they may provide a clue as to how to answer the skipped questions.

If later on, you still can't answer the skipped ones . . . ***Guess.*** The only penalty for guessing is that you *might* get it wrong. Only one thing is certain; if you don't put anything down, you will get it wrong!

3. Turn the question into a statement. Look at the way the questions are worded. The syntax of the question usually provides a clue. Does it seem more familiar as a statement rather than as a question? Does it sound strange?

By turning a question into a statement, you may be able to spot if an answer sounds right, and it may also trigger memories of material you have read.

4. Look for hidden clues. It's actually very difficult to compose multiple-foil (choice) questions without giving away part of the answer in the options presented.

In most multiple-choice questions you can often readily eliminate one or two of the potential answers. This leaves you with only two real possibilities and automatically your odds go to Fifty-Fifty for very little work.

5. Trust your instincts. For every fact that you have read, you subconsciously retain something of that knowledge. On questions that you aren't really certain about, go with your basic instincts. **Your first impression on how to answer a question is usually correct.**

6. Mark your answers directly on the test booklet. Don't bother trying to fill in the optical scan sheet on the first pass through the test.

Just be very careful not to miss-mark your answers when you eventually transcribe them to the scan sheet.

7. Watch the clock! You have a set amount of time to answer the questions. Don't get bogged down trying to answer a single question at the expense of 10 questions you can more readily answer.

Sample Test

Choose the correct response.

1. **C'est un beau chemisier…**

   A. Blanche

   B. Blanc

   C. Blancs

   D. Blanches

2. **Les _____ étaient fantastiques.**

   A. Récitals

   B. Recitaux

   C. Recital

   D. Reciteaux

3. **Ce sont ____, Jeanne et Robert, qui doivent réparer la porte.**

   A. Leur

   B. Les

   C. Elles

   D. Eux

4. **Après tout ton travail, je vais ___donner un jour de congé.**

   A. Que

   B. Le

   C. te

   D. Lui

5. **C'est l'école ____ j'ai fréquentée.**

   A laquelle

   B. Qui

   C. Que

   D. De quoi

6. **Tu ne comprends pas ____ je disais?**

   A. Ce dont

   B. De qui

   C. Ce que

   D. Ce quoi

7. **Veux-tu emprunter la voiture de ton père ou**

   A. La mienne

   B. Moi

   C. Le mien

   D. Le tien

8. De ces deux disques, ____ a-t-il choisi?

A. Quel

B. Qu'

C. Laquelle

D. Lequel

9. **Select the correct pronoun combination to replace the underlined words.**

Je vais montrer mes photos à ma soeur. Je vais ____ montrer.

A. La leur

B. Le leur

C. Lui en

D. Les lui

10. Est-ce qu'il te donne de l'argent? Oui, il ____ donne.

A. M'en

B. Vous le

C. Me le

D. T'en

11. As-tu écrit <u>des poèmes à ta petite amie</u>? Oui, je_____ ai ecrit.

A. Les y

B. Lui en

C. L'en

D. Les lui

12. Il y a ____ marché, en particulier, près de chez moi.

A. Le

B. Du

C. La

D. Un

13. Avez-vous jamais mangé ____ bouillabaisse?

A. Du

B. De la

C. La

D. De

14. Il y a beaucoup de palais ____ Vienne.

A. En

B. Au

C. A

D. A la

15. J'ai passé tout l'été ____ Mexique.

   A. Au

   B. A la

   C. De

   D. A

16. Choose the correct placement and agreement of the adjectives.

   Apportez des galettes! (petit, sec)

   A. --De petits secs galettes.

   B. --De petites galettes sèches.

   C. --De petites sèches alettes.

   D. --De petits galettes secs.

17. Select the correct response to complete the sentence.

   Vos notes sont ____ que les miennes.

   A. Meilleurs

   B. Meilleures

   C. Mieux

   D. Les mieux

18. C'est la robe la plus chère ___ boutique.

   A. De la

   B. Dans

   C. En la

   D. Du

19. Select the correct response.

   Mes parents ont conduit ____voiture en vacances.

   A. Ses

   B. Son

   C. Leur

   D. Leurs

20. Select the correct response.

   ____hors-d'oeuvre sont délicieux.

   A. Cet

   B. Ces

   C. Cette

   D. Ce

21. **Identify the correct demonstrative.**

    A. Cette

    B. Le leur

    C. Ce que

    D. Celui dont

22. **Select the correct form of the adverb for the adjective constant.**

    A. Constantement

    B. Constanment

    C. Consamment

    D. Constamment

23. **Which of the following adverbs is <u>not</u> correct.**

    A. Énormément

    B. Gentillement

    C. Doucement

    D. Follement

24. **Choose the verb that best completes the sentence.**

    Voici une demi-heure que je vous ____.

    A. Attende

    B. Attends

    C. Attendais

    D. Attendez

25. **Select the verb that best completes the sentence.**

    Je te donnerai ma réponse quand je te ____.

    A. Reverrai

    B. Revois

    C. Reverrais

    D. Reverras

26. **Select the verb that best completes the sentence.**

    On les ____ cinq minutes hier soir.

    A. A applaudis

    B. Applauddissait

    C. Applaudirent

    D. Ont applaudi

27. Select the correct verbs that best complete the sentence.

Je ____chez moi, parce que j' ____malade.

A. Etais reste - avais

B. Suis resté - étais

C. Ai reste - etais

D. Ai reste - avais

28. Select the correct response.

Si tu ____ des économies, tu pourrais acheter une nouvelle voiture

A. Faisais

B. Feras

C. Fais

D. Ferais

29. Si'l neigeait, nous ____ faire du ski.

A. Pourrions

B. Aurions pu

C. Puissions

D. Avons pu

30. Select the correct form of the verb.

Bien qu'ils ____riches, ils ne sont pas heureux.

A. Soient

B. Sont

C. Seront

D. Etaient

31. Select the correct response.

N'a-t-elle jamais plus vu un film qui lui ____?

A. Plaît

B. Plaire

C. Plaisent

D. Plaise

32. Select the correct verb form.

Richelieu ____ ministre sous deux rois.

A. Était

B. Eut

C. Fut

D. A été

33. **Select the best response.**

    Maman, j'ai faim, _____ le dîner, s'il te plaît!

    A. Prépare

    B. Prepares

    C. Preparer

    D. Preparez

34. **Which sentence is an example of the passive voice?**

    A. On s'amusait au bal.

    B. Elles se sont parlé à la maison.

    C. Nous étions corrigés par le professeur.

    D. Je me suis regardé dans la glace.

35. **Select the correct response.**

    _____ mal au dos, il ne pouvait lever la boîte.

    A. Avoir

    B. Etant

    C. Ayant

    D. Il y a eu

36. **Identify the past participle.**

    A. Punit

    B. Rendit

    C. Construit

    D. Meurt

37. **Select the correct response.**

    Après ____, Marie a pris du café et a mangé un croissant.

    A. S'était habillée

    B. S'a habille

    C. S'avoir habille

    D. S'être habillée

38. **Select the correct response.**

    Sans ____, il a pris 125F dans mon portefeuille.

    A. Me demander

    B. M'a demandé

    C. Me demande

    D. Me demandait

39. **Which of the following is a reciprocal verb construction?**

    A. Nous nous sommes vus.

    B. Ils se sont impatientés.

    C. Vous vous en êtes allés.

    D. Ils se sont ennuyés.

40. **Select the correct response.**

    Ton frère et toi ____ beaucoup de lait.

    A. Boit

    B. Buvez

    C. Boivent

    D. Bois

41. **Select the correct response.**

    De toutes nos plages en Floride, ____ est la plus belle.

    A. Celles-ci

    B. Ceux-ci

    C. Celle-là

    D. Celui-ci

42. **Select the best response.**

    Celles-ci ne sont pas les photos que Jean a_____.

    A. Développé

    B. Développés

    C. Développée

    D. Développées

43. **Select the best response.**
    Marie et Anne y étaient ____ avant d'écouter les annonces.

    A. Arrivé

    B. Arrivés

    C. Arrivées

    D. Arrivée

44. **Select the correct response.**

    Pourquoi se sont-ils _____ quand ils se sont parlé chaque jour?

    A. Ecrit

    B. Ecrite

    C. Ecrites

    D. Ecrits

45. To which dialect is the french language of today most closely related?

   A. La langue d'oc

   B. La langue d'oïl

   C. La langue romaine

   D. La romanche

46. Where in Paris do you go to see XIXth Century art?

   A. The Carnavalet Museum

   B. The Picasso Museum

   C. The Orsay Museum

   D. The Louvre

47. Where would you be if you were to read the following?

   Les colis internationaux- une gamme complète de services "sur mesure".

   A. La poste

   B. L'hôtel

   C. La banque

   D. Le restaurant

48. Which means of travel would you be using by reading the following?

   Du 15 juillet au 2 septembre, Les horaires modifiés - pour améliorer votre confort et la qualité du service, la SNCF effectuera des travaux sur les voies.

   A. En avion

   B. En train

   C. En autobus

   D. En bateau

49. Where would you be visiting if you heard this explanation?

   La zone viticole déterminée par la nature d'un sous-sol crayeux spécifique, est officiellement délimitée par la loi française: elle couvre 34.000 ha dont plus de 25.000 sont plantés en vignes.

   A. Une ferme historique en Provence.

   B. Un observatoire

   C. Le bureau agricole

   D. Un vignoble champenois

50. **After reading the following ads, what might you be convinced to do?**

-La sécurité d'un service de remboursement mondial
-L'universalité d'un moyen de paiement international
-Le choix de la devise qui vous convient

A. Acheter des chèques de voyage

B. Acheter des vêtements d'une compagnie internationale

C. Obtenir un prêt auprès d'une banque

D. Envoyer un paquet outre-mer

51. **Look at the schedule and select the correct response.**

N du TGV	736
Grenoble	D
10.44	
Lyon-Part-Dieu	D
12.00	
Macon-TGV	D
Le Creusot-TGV	D
Paris-Gare de Lyon	A
14.04	

Combien d'heures dure le voyage du départ à l'arrivée?

A. 2h 45

B. 2h 20

C. 3h 20

D. 4h 20

52. **How many francs will you spend to go 1st class, round trip, from Strasbourg to Lyon?**

A. 419F

B. 355F

C. 710F

D. 774F

53. **How long does this exposition in Paris last?**

Exposition les peintres et les sculpteurs naïfs de Louisiane Exposition de peintres et de sculpteurs de pays Caju n. Du 20/6/89 au 14/07/89

A. 1 week

B. 2 weeks

C. 3 weeks

D. 4 weeks

54. **What is another term referring to the leisure activity of Pétanque?**

A. La pelote

B. Le football

C. Le jeu de boules

D. Un jeu de cartes

55. **For which profession does one prepare at l'Ecole Normale Supérieure?**

    A. Professeur de l'enseignement secondaire

    B. Ingénieur civil

    C. Secrétaire international

    D. Médecin

56. **Which political party did the former president, François Mitterand renew?**

    A. Le parti gaulliste

    B. Le parti démocratique

    C. Le parti communiste

    D. Le parti socialiste

57. **Which of these territories was the first state ruled by African descendants, to gain its independence from France?**

    A. La Martinique

    B. Haïti

    C. La Guadeloupe

    D. La Mauritanie

58. **Select the best translation of the underlined word.**

    Cet avocat méchant n'a pas bien défendu ce client qui était le mari de sa maîtresse.

    A. Bad

    B. Mean

    C. Spiteful

    D. Impolite

59. **Select the correct order of directions for using a Télécarte in France.**

    1. Composer votre numéro
    2. Introduire la carte
    3. Décrocher
    4. Communication
    5. Attendre la tonalité

    A. 2,3,1,5,4

    B. 3,2,5,1,4

    C. 1,3,2,5,4

    D. 3,5,2,1,4

60. **Select the best translation for the following.**

    Il me reste 25f.

    A. I have 25f left.

    B. He leaves me 25f.

    C. There remains 25f.

    D. He owes me 25f.

61. **Select the best translation for the following.**

You have 2 months until the night before departure to purchase the ticket.

A. Il y a 2 mois que tu as avant la veille d'acheter ton billet.

B. Pendant 2 mois, tu peux acheter ton billet avant le départ.

C. L'achat de billet est possible depuis 2 mois jusqu'à la veille du départ.

D. On peut acheter un billet la veille du départ,dans 2 mois.

62. **Select the correct translation.**

Elle n'en a pas les moyens.

A. She doesn't know the way.

B. It didn't mean anything.

C. She can't afford it.

D. She doesn't have the ability.

63. **Select the response which is not a French cognate.**

A. Blesser

B. Pâlir

C. Respirer

D. Choquer

64. **Select the response that is not a French cognate.**

A. La chirurgie

B. La pilule

C. La lecture

D. Le vertige

65. **Select the correct translation.**

Yesterday I drank some milk.

A. Hier je buvais du lait.

B. Hier j'avais bu du lait.

C. Hier j'ai bu du lait.

D. Hier je boivais du lait.

66. **Select the appropriate translation.**

That wouldn't have pleased anyone.

A. Cela n'aurait plu à personne.

B. Personne n'aurait plu à cela.

C. Cela n'aurait plu personne.

D. Cela personne n'aurait plu.

67. Select the correct response to the following question.

Il ne pleut guère en été, n'est-ce pas?

A. Oui, il pleut souvent.

B. Si, il pleut tout l'été.

C. Oui, il ne pleut guère.

D. Si, il ne pleut guère.

La Culture

68. Which French king proclaimed the Edit of Nantes.

A. Louis IX

B. Louis XI

C. Louis XIII

D. Henry IV

69. Which king of France was responsible for bringing the Renaissance to France?

A. François I

B. Louis XIII

C. Louis XI

D. Henri II

70. Who founded the Académie Française?

A. Louis XV

B. Mazarin

C. Louis XVI

D. Richelieu

71. The costly wars, extravagant taste and colonization of this king, led up to the French Revolution.

A. Louis XIV

B. Louis XV

C. Louis XVI

D. Louis XIII

72. This person was responsible for the Reign of Terror.

A. Robespierre

B. Marie- Antoinette

C. Louis XIV

D. Richelieu

73. **This leader of France is credited with giving France a new civil code, the Banque de France, and new schools called "lycées".**

   A. Louis XVIII

   B. Louis- Philippe

   C. Richelieu

   D. Napoléon I

74. **He was the last king to govern France.**

   A. Louis XVIII

   B. Louis- Philippe

   C. Napoléon III

   D. Charles X

75. **Which provinces were lost to Germany after the Franco-Prussian war?**

   A. Alsace and Lorraine

   B. Lorraine and Savoie

   C. Bourgogne and Champagne

   D. Alsace and Savoie

76. **This leader of the French army during WWII became president of the 5th Republic.**

   A. Général Pétain

   B. Général de Gaulle

   C. Général Foch

   D. Général Joffre

77. **In which province is Chamonix located?**

   A. Provence

   B. Savoie

   C. Lorraine

   D. Languedoc

78. **In which province is Brest located?**

   A. Languedoc

   B. Bretagne

   C. Normandie

   D. Picardie

79. **Which mountains separate France from Switzerland.**

   A. Les Alpes

   B. Les Pyrénées

   C. Le Jura

   D. Les Vosges

80. Which river is the longest in France, along which are many châteaux?

A. La Seine

B. La Garonne

C. Le Rhône

D. La Loire

81. Which island was the retreat for the painter Gauguin?

A. La Martinique

B. Tahiti

C. Haïti

D. La Guyane Française

82. Which is the next most important person in the French government after the president?

A. Le Maire de Paris

B. Le Premier Ministre

C. Le Consul Général

D. Le Député à l'Assemblée Nationale

83. How long does France's presidential term last?

A. 7 ans

B. 5 ans

C. 4 ans

D. 3 ans

84. Which of the following allows you to do your banking and call your friends?

A. La Banque Nationale de Paris

B. Le Minitel

C. Le TGV

D. Le RER

85. Léopold Senghor, born African, raised in France, was the 1st president of this country.

A. La Mauritanie

B. L'Algérie

C. Le Sénégal

D. Le Libéria

86. **Which of the following is one of the most important exports of France?**

   A. Le fromage.

   B. Le pétrole

   C. Le coton

   D. Le cacao

87. **Which of the following was a famous French film director and also married to Candice Bergen?**

   A. Francois Truffaut

   B. Alain Resnais

   C. Louis Malle

   D. Claude Lelouch

88. **Which of the following is the current president of France (1995)?**

   A. Francois Mitterand

   B. Pierre Mauroy

   C. Jacques Chirac

   D. Michel Rocard

89. **Which of the following singers is popular in the U.S., Canada, and France?**

   A. Céline Dion

   B. Brigitte Bardot

   C. Mireille Mathieu

   D. Chantal Goya

90. **Which French author was voted the most popular among the French according to Le Figaro Magazine?**

   A. Victor Hugo

   B. Rabelais

   C. Corneille

   D. Molière

91. **Which of the following past times are most similar in the U.S. and France?**

   A. Food

   B. Politics

   C. Sports

   D. Music

92. In which country do they celebrate the feast of Jean-Baptiste, le 24 juin?

   A. Canada

   B. Martinique

   C. France

   D. Guadeloupe

Literature

93. Which is the 1st document written in old French?

   A. Chanson de Roland

   B. Le Roman de Renard

   C. Les Miracles et Mystères

   D. Les Serments de Strasbourg

94. Who was the head of the group of 7 poets called the Pléiade?

   A. François Villon

   B. Malherbe

   C. Charles d'Orléans

   D. Pierre de Ronsard

95. Which of the following was the main literary movement of the 17th century?

   A. Le Romantisme

   B. Le Classicisme

   C. Le Réalisme

   D. L'Impressionisme

96. Which of the following wrote the famous "Maximes"?

   A. Le duc de La Rochefoucauld

   B. Mme de Sévigné

   C. La Bruyère

   D. René Descarts

97. Who is famous for the following quote?

   "Je pense, donc je suis."

   A. Montesquieu

   B. Descartes

   C. Voltaire

   D. Pascal

98. **Which is the name for the literary style, began in the salons, with emphasis on preciseness of words.**

    A. La préciosité

    B. La clarté

    C. La satire

    D. L'ordre

99. **Which of the following wrote Le Rouge et le Noir - a psychological novel?**

    A. Alphonse de Lamartine

    B. Honoré de Balzac

    C. Stendhal

    D. Châteaubriand

100. **In which of the following stories does Gustave Flaubert give us a picture of life in a small Normandy town?**

    A. La Parure

    B. Eugénie Grandet

    C. Madame Bovary

    D. René

101. **Which of the following exemplifies the sentiment of 19th century literature?**

    A. La vérité

    B. Le malaise

    C. La tradition classique

    D. La discipline

102. **Which of the following was the head of the existentialist movement?**

    A. Anatole France

    B. Jean Paul Sartre

    C. Albert Camus

    D. Antoine de St. Exupéry

103. **Which of the following wrote La Peste and La Chute?**

    A. Anatole France

    B. Jean-Paul Sartre

    C. Camus

    D. Jean Anouilh

104. **Which cartoon is no longer published in French newspapers?**

    A. Tintin

    B. Peanuts

    C. Family Circus

    D. Astérix

105. In the French song, Sur le Pont d'Avignon, what are the men and ladies doing?

    A. ils dansent

    B. ils chantent

    C. ils regardent les bateaux

    D. ils racontent des histories

106. Which of the following sculpted le Penseur?

    A. Picasso

    B. Rodin

    C. Aristide Maillol

    D. Jean-Antoine Houdon

107. Which of the following composed Au Clair de la Lune?

    A. Bizet

    B. Debussy

    C. Ravel

    D. Saint Saëns

108. Which of the following is known for his painting of dancers at the Opera?

    A. Renoir

    B. Manet

    C. Cézanne

    D. Degas

109. Which of the following began the style of Pointillisme?

    A. Claude Monet

    B. Edouard Manet

    C. Georges Seurat

    E. Auguste Renoir

Pedagogy

110. Which of the following activities will help the students most easily in remembering the placement of direct/indirect objects?

    A. Singing - Au Clair de la Lune

    B. Writing activities

    C. Partner practice

    D. Listening to a story

111. What is a fun way to assess knowledge of verb structures?

    A. Conjugating verbs

    B. Writing activities

    C. Play 20 questions

    D. Play dice-verb game with partner

112. **What is an easy way to help build reading comprehension and vocabulary retention at the first level?**

    A. Cognate instruction

    B. Flash cards

    C. Partner practice

    D. Translation

113. **Which of the following would best test a student's reading comprehension in French III?**

    A. Ask student questions

    B. Have student translate selection

    C. Have student make up questions

    D. Have student write a resume of the selection

114. **Which method would best teach students the art of letter writing?**

    A. Translating sentences

    B. French pen pals

    C. Write notes in French to friends in class

    D. Copy example letters from the text

115. **Which method will allow assessment of students of written skills already learned?**

    A. Guided composition

    B. Translation sentences

    C. Write a resume of story

    D. Writing exercises

116. **Select the activity best suited to practice speaking skills.**

    A. Partner practice

    B. Repeat after the teacher

    C. Read aloud

    D. Listen to tape then record separately the same words selection.

117. **Which method is best for teaching listening skills?**

    A. Listening to French cassettes

    B. Partner practice

    C. Constant use of French by teacher in classroom

    D. Giving dictations to students

118. **Which game would be fun to practice listening skills?**

A. Pictionary

B. Jeopardy in French

C. Partner practice

D. 20 Questions

119. **Select the activity best suited to learning culture.**

A. Global bingo

B. Show and tell

C. Read book

D. Show a movie

120. **Which would not be appropriate for teaching and explaining culture?**

A. Show and tell

B. Pictionary

C. Movie

D. Global Bingo

Answer Key

1. B	31. D	61. C	91. D
2. A	32. C	62. C	92. A
3. D	33. A	63. A	93. D
4. C	34. C	64. C	94. D
5. A	35. C	65. C	95. B
6. C	36. C	66. A	96. A
7. A	37. D	67. B	97. B
8. D	38. A	68. D	98. A
9. D	39. A	69. A	99. C
10. A	40. B	70. D	100. C
11. B	41. C	71. B	101. B
12. D	42. D	72. A	102. B
13. B	43. C	73. D	103. C
14. C	44. A	74. B	104. D
15. A	45. B	75. A	105. A
16. B	46. C	76. B	106. B
17. B	47. A	77. B	107. B
18. A	48. B	78. B	108. D
19. C	49. D	79. C	109. C
20. B	50. A	80. D	110. A
21. A	51. C	81. B	111. D
22. D	52. B	82. B	112. A
23. B	53. C	83. B	113. D
24. B	54. C	84. B	114. B
25. A	55. A	85. C	115. A
26. A	56. D	86. A	116. D
27. B	57. B	87. C	117. C
28. A	58. C	88. C	118. D
29. A	59. B	89. A	119. B
30. A	60. A	90. A	120. B

Rationales with Sample Questions

Writing

1. **Choose the correct response.**

   C'est un beau chemisier.

   A. Blanche

   B. Blanc

   C. Blancs

   D. Blanches

Answer B is the right answer: Blanc. Chemisier is a masculine noun, and there is only one, which leaves all of the other answers out (Blanche is feminine, Blanches is feminine plural, and Blancs is masculine, but plural).

2. **Les _____ étaient fantastiques.**

   A. Récitals

   B. Récitaux

   C. Récital

   D. Réciteaux

Answer A is the right answer. Most nouns ending with –al in the masculine singular become –aux in the plural, but such is not the case of Recital. B is therefore erroneous, C is in the singular, and D applies a rule used in nouns such as "Rideau", which does not apply to "Recital".

3. **Ce sont ____, Jeanne et Robert, qui doivent réparer la porte.**

   A. Leur

   B. Les

   C. Elles

Answer D, which is a disjunctive pronoun used after the verbe "Etre". C is a disjunctive pronoun as well, but it is a feminine. A is an indirect object pronoun used with verbs of communication with the preposition "à" (Donner à, Parler à, ...) and B is a direct object pronoun.

4. **Après tout votre travail, je vais ___donner un jour de congé.**

   A. Que

   B. Le

   C. te

   D. Lui

Answer C is an indirect object pronoun modifying the verb "Donner"; the rule of parallelism is respected here ("ton" and "te"). A is impossible: it is a relative pronoun demanding an antecedent (such as: je vois le livre QUE je t'ai donné). B is a direct object pronoun and cannot modify the verb "Donner", which demands an indirect object pronoun.

5. C'est l'école _____ j'ai fréquentée.

    A A laquelle

    B. Qui

    C. Que

    D. De quoi

Answer C The relative pronoun "que" is the appropriate one because the verb "fréquenter" is transitive direct, and the direct object " école " being a thing, "qui" would not fit here; therefore, the only choice is "que".

6. Tu ne comprends pas _____ je disais?

    A. Ce dont

    B. De qui

    C. Ce que

    D. Ce quoi

Answer C: a direct object relative pronoun modifying "Disais". To have A as an answer, we should have an indirect verb requiring the preposition "de": Tu ne comprends pas CE DONT je parlais, for instance (verb "Parler de"). It is the same case with B, but you would have to have a person and not a thing: Tu ne comprends pas De Qui je parlais. As for D, Quoi always comes immediately after "à" or "de", which isn't the case here.

7. Veux-tu emprunter la voiture de ton père ou

    A. La mienne

    B. Moi

    C. Le mien

    D. Le tien

Answer A: it is a feminine possessive pronoun replacing "Ma voiture". B would not make sense here since you do not want to borrow me (Moi). C would be fine, except that it is a masculine and we need a feminine pronoun. D is impossible: why would you need to borrow your own car, plus it is a masculine anyway.

8. De ces deux disques, _____ a-t-il choisi?

    A. Quel

    B. Qu'

    C. Laquelle

    D. Lequel

D is right here: Lequel is either a relative pronoun coming after a preposition (l'ami avec lequel je parle), or an interrogative pronoun, which is needed here. A is an interrogative, but an adjective: it demands a noun (Quel disque a-t-il choisi?). B is not specific enough. C is an interrogative pronoun, but it is feminine and Disque is masculine.

9. **Select the correct pronoun combination to replace the underlined words.**

Je vais montrer <u>mes photos</u> <u>à ma soeur</u>. Je vais ____ montrer.

A. La leur

B. Le leur

C. Lui en

D. Les lui

D is the right answer: "Les" replaces "Mes photos", "Lui" replaces "A ma soeur". "Mes photos" is a direct object, therefore it has to be replaced with a direct object pronoun. "A ma soeur", on the other hand, is indirect, and has to be replaced by "Lui". A cannot work here: "La" is singular, and "Leur" is plural: there is more than one photo, but only one "Soeur". B is exactly the same as A, except that "La" is replaced with "Le", which would be one masculine thing and we have more than one photo. C does have the right indirect pronoun ("Lui"), but the wrong direct object pronoun: "En" replaces a direct object only when it is introduced by an indefinite article (Un, Une, Des), a partitive article (Du, De la,, De l'), or an expression of quantity (Beaucoup de, Peu de, Une tranche de, etc.). Here, "Photos" is introduced by a possessive adjective.
In addition, using the possessive in a question is quite illogical. Rather, the demonstrative adjective "ces" is the only plausible alternative.

10. Est-ce qu'il te donne de l'argent? Oui, il ____ donne.

A. M'en

B. Vous le

C. Me le

D. T'en

A is the right answer. "M'" is the indirect object pronoun for the verb "Donne", and "En" is the direct object. "En" here replaces the direct object "De l'argent", where the noun is introduced by a partitive (see above). B is impossible: "Vous" would imply that the question was asked using "Vous", whereas it was asked using "Te". Therefore, the other person answers using "M'" . "Le" is impossible as a direct object, since "De l'" is used to introduce "Argent". C cannot be used: We have just seen that "Le" is wrong here. As far as D is concerned, it doesn't work since the person is answering a question about him/herself.

11. **As-tu écrit <u>des poèmes</u> <u>à ta petite amie</u>? Oui, je_____ ai ecrit.**

    A. Les y

    B. Lui en

    C. L'en

    D. Les lui

In the question here, we have a direct object ("Des poemes") and an indirect one ("A ta petite amie"). B is the right answer, since "Lui" replaces "A ma petite amie" and "En" replaces "Des poèmes": "En" is used here since "Poèmes" is introduced by an indefinite article ("Des"). A is wrong: "Les" cannot replace "Des poèmes". Y is never used as an indirect object pronoun. In C, "L'" cannot be used for two reasons: first because we have to have "En" (indefinite article), second because an indirect pronoun never contracts to "L'" anyway. D does not work simply because as we just saw, "Des poèmes" has to be replaced by "En".

12. **Il y a ____ marché, en particulier, près de chez moi.**

    A. Le

    B. Du

    C. La

    D. Un

The correct answer is D: there is "a" market, "Un" marché. We need here an indefinite article, since it is not a specific market. A would be used just for this: if we had a specific market, then we would use the definite article "Le". But it is not the case. B is a partitive article, used when we want to express part of something (Part-itive): we are not expressing anything about part of a market, plus the partitive is used mainly for food –with some exceptions: De la chance, for example. C is like A, except it is in the feminine.

13. Avez-vous jamais mangé
    _____ bouillabaisse?

    A. Du

    B. De la

    C. La

    E. De

The correct answer is B: "De la", which is a partitive article. We are not talking about eating all of the bouillabaisse in the world (in which case we would use C, the definite article "La"), but some of it, which the partitive expresses. A is not right, even though it is a partitive, because it is masculine. D is not correct: "De" is not an article of any kind, except a partitive in the negative (for instance: Il mange de la bouillabaisse, il ne mange pas de bouillabaisse).

14. Il y a beaucoup de palais
    _____ Vienne.

    A. En

    B. Au

    C. à

    D. A la

C is correct: the preposition "A" is used with cities. "En" is used for countries whose names end with an "e", "Au" for countries whose names end with another letter. As for D, it is neither used for cities, nor for countries.

15. J'ai passé tout l'été _____
    Mexique.

    A. au

    B. A la

    C. De

    D. A

A is right! Unfortunately, the French language just loves exceptions: "En" is used for countries ending in "e" –feminine countries-, and "Au" for countries ending with another letter – masculine countries-. Alas, some countries ending with "e" are masculine, therefore requiring the preposition "Au": Le Mexique, Le Zaire, Le Cambodge, and… Le Maine (etat americain). B is wrong: "A la" is used for small island (A la Jamaique, for example). De is never used for such things and simply does not make sense here. D is wrong too: as we saw, "A" is used for cities.

16. **Choose the correct placement and agreement of the adjectives.**

Apportez des galettes! (petit, sec)

A. --De petits secs galettes.

B. --De petites galettes sèches.

C. --De petites sèches galettes.

D. --De petits galettes secs.

B is the right answer. In French, BANGS adjectives come before the noun: they express Beauty (or lack thereof), Age, Numbers, Goodness (or badness), Size ("BANGS"). All other adjectives go after the noun: so here, petit comes first, and sec after the noun. Petit will be "Petites" since "Galettes" is feminine plural, "Sec" will be "Seches" and will come after the noun. A has both the gender wrong, and the placement of "Secs" is wrong too. C would be right if it wasn't for the placement of "Seches". D would be right too, except that the gender is wrong.

17. **Select the correct response to complete the sentence.**

Vos notes sont ____ que les miennes.

A. Meilleurs

B. Meilleures

C. Mieux

D. Les mieux

B is correct. Indeed, we need a comparative here: "Meilleures" is such a thing, in the feminine plural, as "Notes" demands. A would be right, but the gender is wrong. As far as C is concerned, "Mieux" is indeed a comparative, but it is the comparative of an adverb (and we all know that adverbs modifiy verbs or adjectives). The "Notes" are "Bonnes" and "Meilleures", not "Bien" and "Mieux". "Meilleur" is the comparative of an adjective, the adjective "Bon".As far as D is concerned, there are two reasons why it cannot work here: first "Mieux" is used, and second "Les mieux" is used, which is a superlative for "Mieux". We need a comparative here, not a superlative.

18. C'est la robe la plus chère
        ___ boutique.

   A. de la

   B. Dans

   C. En la

   D. Du

Here, A is right. "La plus chère"
is a superlative, which in French
entails the use of the preposition
"De". B is wrong, since it does
not have the preposition "De".
This is also the case with C, which
is wrong in itself anyway: "En la"
is never used. D could be right if
"Boutique" were masculine (it
does use the preposition "De": la
plus chere "de le" boutique, Du),
but the gender is wrong.

19. Select the correct response.

   Mes parents ont conduit
   ____voiture en vacances.

   A. Ses

   B. Son

   C. Leur

   D. Leurs

C is right. We need a possessive
adjective here, and "Leur"
corresponds to the person "Ils"
(Mes parents). There is only one
"Voiture", so "Leur" is right. A
cannot work here: it is the wrong
possessive adjective,
corresponding to "Il" ou "Elle",
and "Mes parents" are "Ils". So it
is wrong. Furthermore, "Ses"
implies only one possessor, and
several things possessed: just the
opposite of what we have here. B
also refers to one possessor, plus
the gender is wrong. D would be
right if They ("Ils", mes parents)
possessed more than one car.

20. Select the correct response.

_____hors-d'oeuvre sont délicieux.

A. Cet

B. Ces

C. Cette

D. Ce

B is right. Hors d'oeuvre is plural, even though there is no "s" after "oeuvre". Therefore, "Ces" is the right answer. "Cet" would work if the noun were singular, and also if the "H" were not "aspiré" (meaning it cannot be preceded by a consonant, unlike most nouns starting with "H". C is impossible because of the plural and the gender, and Ce is in the singular.

21. Identify the demonstrative.

A. Cette

B. Le leur

C. Ce que

D. Celui dont

A is the correct answer. D is the Demonstrative Pronoun. Here, it is accompanied by the relative pronoun "Dont." A is a demonstrative, but it is a demonstrative adjective, meaning that it has to have a noun with it: cette voiture, for example. Unlike an adjective, a pronoun can be subject or object. B is a pronoun, but it is a possessive pronoun. C is also a pronoun, but it is a relative pronoun whose particularity is that it does not have an antecedent: "Ecoutez ce que je dis", for example.

22. **Select the correct form of the adverb for the adjective constant.**

A. Constantement

B. Constanment

C. Consamment

D. Constamment

D is right. In order to find the adverb corresponding to an adjective, you add "-ment" to it if it ends with an "e" or another vowell, and "-ment" to its feminine if it ends with a consonant. As far as adjectives in "-ent" and "-ant" are concerned, you take off the ending (-ent or –ant) and add "-emment" to those in "-ent", and "-amment-" to those in "-ant". Therefore, "Constamment" is right, since the adjective is "Constant".

23. **Which of the following adverbs is not correct.**

A. Énormément

B. Gentillement

C. Doucement

D. Follement

B is not correct. Even though you add "-ment" to the feminine form of an adjective ending with a consonant in the masculine, "Gentil" is an exception: the adverb is "Gentiment". A illustrates the rule of adding "-ment" to adjectives ending in "-e" in the masculine singular, and C illustrates the rule of adding "-ment" to the feminine of an adjective ending with a consonant in the masculine singular: Doux, feminine Douce, adverb Doucement. Fou is an exception, ending with a vowel but forming its adverb on the feminine.

24. Choose the verb that best completes the sentence.

Voici une demi-heure que je vous ____.

A. Attende

B. Attends

C. Attendais

D. Attendez

The correct answer is B: an action that started in the past but which is still going on is described in the present: "Il y a/Voici/Voila une heure que je vous attends". A is wrong simply because it is the present subjunctive. C is wrong because of the rule expressed above, the action is still going on so there is no reason to use the past. D is an interesting mistake: it mixes up the subject and the object of the verb: "Je vous attends". "Je" is the subject, and "Vous" is the direct object. D shows that the speaker believes the object is actually the subject.

completes the sentence.

Je te donnerai ma réponse quand je te ____.

A. Reverrai

B. Revois

C. Reverrais

D. Reverras

A is correct. In French, when the main clause is in the future ("Je te donnerai"), the subordinate clause ("Quand je te reverrai") has to be in the future as well. This is why B is incorrect. C is wrong because the verb ("Reverrais") is in the conditional, which is inappropirate in this sentence. D is wrong too, because "I" am the one who will see you again ("Je te reverrai"), and the form of Revoir here ("Reverras") is in the "Tu" form.

25. Select the verb that best

26. Select the verb that best completes the sentence.

On les ____ cinq minutes hier soir.

A. A applaudis

B. Applauddissait

C. Applaudirent

D. Ont applaudi

A is the right answer: the Passé-Composé, among other things, describes a definite period of time in the past, here "Cinq minutes". B is in the Imparfait, a tense which often requires another clause in the past in order to be used. For example, we could have: "On les applaudissait depuis cinq minutes hier soir quand l'acteur principal est revenu sur scène." C is in the Passé Simple, which could be used here, but "On" is to be conjugated like "il" et "elle", third person singular, not third person plural. D is in the right tense, but has the wrong subject ("Ils ont applaudi"). Furthermore, "Applaudis" has to have a final "s", since the direct object of the verb ("Les") is placed before the verb ("On les a applaudis").

27. Select the correct verbs that best complete the sentence.

Je ____ chez moi, parce que j' ____ malade.

A. Etais resté - avais

B. Suis resté - étais

C. Ai resté - étais

D. Ai resté - avais

B is right: The first action ("Je suis resté chez moi") is in the Passé-Composé. It is the result of the one in the Imparfait, which here is used to describe a background, something that the Imparfait is often used for. A is not possible: "Etais resté" is in the Plus-que-Parfait, which is used to describe an action that happened before another action already in the past. In this sentence, both actions obviously are contemporary. Also, we need "Etais malade" and not "Avais", since "Malade" is an adjective and not a noun. C would work fine if only Rester did not need the verb "Etre", and not "Avoir", in the Passé-Composé. D is impossible, because of the reason explained in C ("Ai resté"), and because of the one explained in A ("Avais").

28. **Select the correct response.**

Si tu ____ des économies, tu pourrais acheter une nouvelle voiture

A. Faisais

B. Feras

C. Fais

D. Ferais

A is correct: in French, with a main clause in the conditional, as is the case here ("Tu pourrais acheter une voiture"), the subordinate clause starting with "Si" demands a verb in the Imparfait (or in the Plus-que-Parfait if the action of the subordinate precedes the action of the main clause in the Present Conditional, but this is not the case here). B is in the Future, which never accompanies a verb in the Present Conditional. C is in the Present of the Indicative, and our main verb here is in the present Conditional: this combination cannot happen. D is in the Present Conditional, and as we have just seen, the action of the subordinate clause has to be in the Imparfait, with a verb in the Present Conditional.

29. **S'il neigeait, nous ____ faire du ski.**

A. Pourrions

B. Aurions pu

C. Puissions

D. Avons pu

A is the correct answer, although B may seem correct, in "si" clauses certain tenses are used depending on verb tense in the main clause. A means that if it had snowed, we now could ski now. B means that if it had snowed, we could have snowed in the past. C is a Present Subjunctive, which is inappropriate here. D is impossible, since it is in the Indicative and we need a verb in the Conditional with this "Si" clause.

30. **Select the correct form of the verb.**

Bien qu'ils ____riches, ils ne sont pas heureux.

A. Soient

B. Sont

C. Seront

D. Etaient

A is correct: the conjunction "Bien que" demands the use of the subjunctive. B is in the Present of the Indicative, therefore it is wrong. C is in the Future: it is wrong too. D is in the past. The past could be used here, but it would have to be a past tense of the Subjunctive, and D uses the Imparfait of the Indicative.

31. **Select the correct response.**

N'a-t-elle jamais plus vu un film qui lui ____?

A. Plaît

B. Plaire

C. Plaisent

D. Plaise

D is in the subjunctive, and it is right. Besides accompanying conjunctions such as Bien que, Quoique, Sans que, Jusqu'a ce que, etc., the subjunctive is also used to express a variety of things, one of them being doubt. Here, the person asking the question doubts whether she has ever seen a film which she likes. A is in the Indicative, which expresses certainty, and we need doubt here. B is an infinitive and does not fit in this sentence. C does use the Subjunctive, but the verb is in the plural and we need the singular here.

32.   **Select the correct verb form.**

Richelieu _____ ministre sous deux rois.

A. Était

B. Eut

C. Fut

D. A été

C is the answer. A is an Imperfect. B is in the Passé-Simple, but it is the verb "Avoir", and here we need "Etre". D is not the Passé-Simple, but the Passé-Composé.

33.   **Select the best response.**

Maman, j'ai faim, _____ le dîner, s'il te plaît!

A. Prépare

B. Prépares

C. Préparer

D. Préparez

A is the best response. "Prépare" is the imperative (Command Form) used for "Tu". B is wrong, because the Imperative of verbs ending in "-er" in the infinitive do not have an "s" in the "tu" form. C is an infinitive and makes no sense here. D isn't right because "Préparez" is the Imperative form for "vous", and the "s'il te plaît" indicates to us that the speaker says "tu" to Maman.

34.   **Which sentence is an example of the passive voice?**

A. On s'amusait au bal.

B. Elles se sont parlé à la maison.

C. Nous étions corrigés par le professeur.

D. Je me suis regardé dans la glace.

C is right. In the active voice, the subject performs the action. For example: They are reading a book. In the passive voice, the subject undergoes the action: A book is being read by them. Therefore C is right: "Nous" are not doing anything, we are being corrected, the one doing the action is the professeur. So A is not the right answer: the subject ("On") is performing the action. This is also the case for B and D.

35. **Select the correct response.**

_____ mal au dos, il ne pouvait pas lever la boîte.

A. Avoir

B. Etant

C. Ayant

D. Il y a eu

C is the right answer: "Ayant" is the Present Participle of "avoir", such as English "having". A cannot be right, the Infinitive not being able to replace such a clause. "Etant" would work, but it is the wrong verb. "Il y a eu" describes an event that happened in the past, it has nothing to do here.

36. **Identify the past participle.**

A. Punit

B. Rendit

C. Construit

D. Meurt

C is the answer, it is the Past Participle of the verb "Construire". A is the third person singular (Il, Elle, On) of the verb "Punir", in the Present. B is also the third person singular of "Rendre" in the Passé-Simple. As far as D is concerned, it is the third person singular of "mourir" in the Present of the Indicative.

37. **Select the correct response.**

Après _____, Marie a pris du café et a mange un croissant.

A. S'était habillée

B. S'a habillé

C. S'avoir habillé

D. S'être habillée

D is the right answer: it is a past infinitive: "Après" demands it. "Après que" would demand a conjugated form, such as: "Après qu'elle se fut habillée, elle a pris du café et un croissant." But this conjunction demands a past infinitive if it is not accompanied by "que": it is also the case of "Sans, Avant de, pour", etc. A would require "que", since it is conjugated. B is impossible: it is conjugated too, first of all, and we have just seen that it does not work here. Moreover, it is conjugated wrongly: a reflexive verb is always accompanied by the verb "Etre", never "Avoir". C is a Past Infinitive, but here too the Auxiliary is wrong, the speaker is using "Avoir" instead of "Etre".

38. **Select the correct response.**

Sans ____, il a pris 125F dans mon portefeuille.

A. Me demander

B. M'a demandé

C. Me demande

D. Me demandait

A is the right answer: "Sans" requires an Infinitive. "Sans que", on the other hand, requires a conjugated form, but in the Subjunctive. Therefore, B is wrong, since "M'a demandé" is in the Indicative, in the Passe-Composé. C would work with "Sans que", since the "Je" form of the Subjunctive of "Demander" is the same as that of the Indicative. D would also require "Sans que", but it is in the Indicative Imperfect anyway, and we need the Subjunctive.

39. **Which of the following is a reciprocal verb construction?**

A. Nous nous sommes vus.

B. Ils se sont impatientés.

C. Vous vous en êtes allés.

D. Ils se sont ennuyés.

A is right. Three kinds of Reflexive verbs exist in French: The "true" reflexives, where the subject and the object of the verb are one and only person. For example: Je me regarde. "Je" is the subject, "Me" the object, and they are but one and the same person. The reciprocals imply that two people are doing something to the other simultaneously: "Ils se regardent", meaning "Il la regarde, Et elle le regarde". These verbs only exist in the plural, as is logical: Se parler, se donner rendez-vous, etc. The third kind is the idiomatic Reflexives: they are Reflexive just because they are: Se presser, S'en aller, etc. Here the only Reciprocal is A.

40. **Select the correct response.**

Ton frère et toi ____ beaucoup de lait.

A. Boit

B. Buvez

C. Boivent

D. Bois

B is correct: "Ton frere et toi" is "Vous".

41. **Select the correct response.**

De toutes nos plages en Floride, ____ est la plus belle.

A. Celles-ci

B. Ceux-ci

C. Celle-là

D. Celui-ci

C is the right answer: it is a feminine singular demonstrative pronoun. A, B and D are demonstrative pronouns as well, but their genders and numbers are wrong.

42. **Select the best response.**

Celles-ci ne sont pas les photos que Jean a_____.

A. Développé

B. Développés

C. Développée

D. Développées

D is correct: "Que" is a relative pronoun whose antecedent is the feminine plural demonstrative pronoun "Celles-ci", and the past participle "Developpées" has to agree with it as a preceding direct object pronoun.

43. **Select the best response.**

Marie et Anne y etaient ____ avant d'ecouter les annonces.

A. Arrivé

B. Arrivés

C. Arrivées

D. Arrivée

C is right: with the verb Etre, the past participle agrees with the subject which is "Marie et Anne."

44. **Select the correct response.**

    Pourquoi se sont-ils _____ quand ils se sont parlé chaque jour?

    A. Ecrit

    B. Ecrite

    C. Ecrites

    D. Ecrits

A is the right answer: even though the object ("Se") precedes the verb, it is an indirect object, with which the past participle never agrees.

45. **To which dialect is the French language of today most closely related?**

    A. La langue d'oc

    B. La langue d'oïl

    C. La langue romaine

    D. La romanche

B is right: in the Middle Ages, "la langue d'oïl" was the vernacular in the Northern part of France, where Paris –the capital- is situated. It is this language which became the language of all of France.

46. **Where in Paris do you go to see XIXth Century art?**

    A. The Carnavalet Museum

    B. The Picasso Museum

    C. The Orsay Museum

    D. The Louvre

The answer is C. This museum was created for the sole purpose of exhibiting XIXth Century art.

47. **Where would you be if you were to read the following?**

    Les colis internationaux- une gamme complète de services "sur mesure".

    A. La poste

    B. L'hôtel

    C. La banque

    D. Le restaurant

A is the right answer: a "colis" is a package that you send by mail.

48. Which means of travel would you be using by reading the following?

Du 15 juillet au 2 septembre, Les horaires modifiés - pour améliorer votre confort et la qualité du service, la SNCF effectuera des travaux sur les voies.

A. En avion

B. En train

C. En autobus

D. En bateau

The correct answer is B: the SNCF stands for "Société Nationale des Chemins de fer Français".

49. Where would you be visiting if you heard this explanation?

La zone viticole déterminée par la nature d'un sous-sol crayeux spécifique, est officiellement délimitée par la loi française: elle couvre 34.000 ha dont plus de 25.000 sont plantés en vignes.

A. Une ferme historique en Provence.

B. Un observatoire

C. Le bureau agricole

D. Un vignoble champenois

The answer is D. The key expression here is "Sous-sol crayeux (chalky soil)", which is typical of the Champagne region.

50. After reading the following ads, what might you be convinced to do?

-La sécurité d'un service de remboursement mondial
-L'universalité d'un moyen de paiement international
-Le choix de la devise qui vous convient

A. Acheter des chèques de voyage

B. Acheter des vêtements d'une compagnie internationale

C. Obtenir un prêt auprès d'une banque

D. Envoyer un paquet outre-mer

51. Look at the schedule and select the correct response.

N du TGV	736
Grenoble	D
10.44	
Lyon-Part-Dieu	D
12.00	
Macon-TGV	D
Le Creusot-TGV	D
Paris-Gare de Lyon	A
14.04	

Combien d'heures dure le voyage du départ à l'arrivée?

A. 2h 45

B. 2h 20

C. 3h 20

D. 4h 20

C is right

52. How may francs will you spend to go 1st class, round trip, from Strasbourg to Lyon?

A. 419F

B. 355F

C. 710F

D. 774F

B is the correct answer

53. How long does this exposition in Paris last?

Exposition LES PEINTRES ET LES SCULPTEURS NAÏFS DE LOUISIANE Exposition de peintres et de sculpteurs du pays Cajun. Du 20/6/89 au 14/07/89

A. 1 week

B. 2 weeks

C. 3 weeks

D. 4 weeks

The answer is C. Dont ever forget that in France, the day goes first, then the month, then the year: 20/6/89 is the 20th of June, 1989.

54. What is another term referring to the leisure activitiy of Pétanque?

A. La pelote

B. Le football

C. Le jeu de boules

D. Un jeu de cartes

C is the right answer. La pétanque is primarily played in the South of France.

55. For which profession does one prepare at l'Ecole Normale Superieure?

A. Professeur de l'enseignement secondaire

B. Ingénieur civil

C. Secrétaire international

D. Médecin

A is right. To become "ingénieur civil", one should attend the "Ecole des Mines". To become "secrétaire international, it is necessary to attend "L' école des sciences politiques". Finally, as is obvious, medical school will allow you to become a physician.

56. Which political party did the former president, François Mitterand renew?

A. Le parti gaulliste

B. Le parti démocratique

C. Le parti communiste

D. Le parti socialiste

D is the right answer. Under the presidency of François Mitterrand, the Socialist Party became the first party in the country.

57. Which of these territories was the first state ruled by African descendants, to gain its independence from France?

A. La Martinique

B. Haïti

C. La Guadeloupe

D. La Mauritanie

B is the correct answer. Haïti was the first modern republic ruled by African descendants. After the rule of King Christophe, a republic was proclaimed.

58. Select the best translation of the underlined word.

Cet avocat <u>méchant</u> n'a pas bien défendu ce client qui était le mari de sa maîtresse.

A. Bad

B. Mean

C. Spiteful

D. Impolite

C would be best: it implies an idea of revenge, which is the case here.

59. Select the correct order of directions for using a Télécarte in France.

1. Composer votre numéro
2. Introduire la carte
3. Décrocher
4. Communication
5. Attendre la tonalité

A. 2,3,1,5,4

B. 3,2,5,1,4

C. 1,3,2,5,4

D. 3,5,2,1,4

B is correct. Remember it for when you go to France!

60. Select the best translation for the following.

Il me reste 25f.

A. I have 25f left.

B. He leaves me 25f.

C. There remains 25f.

D. He owes me 25f.

A is the right answer. B would be a translation for "il me laisse 25f., C would imply that the speaker notices that 25f. remain (we know nothing about the possessor of the money), and D would translate as "il me doit 25f."

61. **Select the best translation for the following.**

You have 2 months until the night before departure to purchase the ticket.

A. Il y a 2 mois que tu as avant la veille d'acheter ton billet.

B. Pendant 2 mois, tu peux acheter ton billet avant le départ.

C. L'achat de billet est possible depuis 2 mois jusqu'à la veille du départ.

D. On peut acheter un billet la veille du départ,dans 2 mois.

C is the right answer.

62. **Select the correct translation.**

Elle n'en a pas les moyens.

A. She doesn't know the way.

B. It didn't mean anything.

C. She can't afford it.

D. She doesn't have the ability.

C is correct. A would be: "Elle ne Connaît pas le chemin", B "Cela ne voulait rien dire, and D means that she is not intellectually or physically able to do something.

63. **Select the response which is not a French cognate.**

A. Blesser

B. Pâlir

C. Respirer

D. Choquer

A is correct: "Blesser"does not mean to bless, but to inflict mental or physical pain to someone.

64. **Select the response that is not a French cognate.**

A. La chirurgie

B. La pilule

C. La lecture

D. Le vertige

The answer is C: "Lecture" does not mean the English word "Lecture", but "reading".

65. **Select the correct translation.**

Yesterday I drank some milk.

A. Hier je buvais du lait.

B. Hier j'avais bu du lait.

C. Hier j'ai bu du lait.

D. Hier je boivais du lait.

The correct answer is C.

66. Select the appropriate translation.

    That wouldn't have pleased anyone.

    A. Cela n'aurait plu à personne.

    B. Personne n'aurait plu à cela.

    C. Cela n'aurait plu personne.

    D. Cela personne n'aurait plu.

A is correct. The other answers do not make sense, either grammatically (C) or because they don't mean anything (B and D).

67. Select the correct response to the following question.

    Il ne pleut guère en été, n'est-ce pas?

    A. Oui, il pleut souvent.

    B. Si, il pleut tout l'été.

    C. Oui, il ne pleut guère.

    D. Si, il ne pleut guère.

The answer is B. When you answer a negative question (Don't you like chocolate, for example) as is the case here, you need to answer with "Si" and not "Oui". However, D makes no sense because it starts with a statement ("Si"), and then turns the sentence into a negative one.

La Culture

68. Which French king proclaimed the Edit of Nantes.

    A. Louis IX

    B. Louis XI

    C. Louis XIII

    D. Henry IV

D is correct. Henry IV was a Protestant, but when he became King of France he had to convert to Catholicism. However, he proclaimed an "Edict", which allowed all the right to be either Protestant or Catholic.

69. Which king of France was responsible for bringing the Renaissance to France?

    A. François I

    B. Louis XIII

    C. Louis XI

    D. Henri II

A is right. François I was a lover of art all of his life, and had a number of Italian artists reside in France such as Leonardo Da Vinci, who spent his last years in France.

70. **Who founded the Academie Francaise?**

A. Louis XV

B. Mazarin

C. Louis XVI

D. Richelieu

D is right. The Académie Française was founded to protect and recognize writers, but also to organize the French language into one centralized language: indeed, at the time, France spoke many dialects. Also, French was to be as close to Latin as possible, and this was another task that the Académie had to perform.

71. **The costly wars, extravagant taste and colonization of this king, led up to the French Revolution.**

A. Louis XIV

B. Louis XV

C. Louis XVI

D. Louis XIII

C is right. Louis XVI came to power in 1774 after Lous XV (nicknamed "Le Bien Aimé). Married to the now infamous Marie-Antoinette, their lavish life style created such hatred among the people of Paris that they revolted, and took the Bastille on July 14, 1789. He was beheaded in 1793, on Place de la Concorde, which had been called "le bien aimé"

72. **This person was responsible for the Reign of Terror.**

A. Robespierre

B. Marie Antoinette

C. Louis XIV

D. Richelieu

A is correct: Robespierre was the most blood thirsty men of the French Revolution. As for Marie-Antoinette (B), she was beheaded. Louis XIV and Richelieu (C and D) had been dead for a long time when the Terror was taking place.

73. This leader of France is credited with giving France a new civil code, the Banque de France, and new schools called "lycées".

   A. Louis XVIII

   B. Louis-Phillipe

   C. Richelieu

   D. Napoléon I

D is the right answer. Napoléon initiated profound changes to the French educational system, some of which are still alive today: for example, the Ecole Polytechnique and the general system of French "Grandes Ecoles" (some of which are Ecole Normale Supérieure or Ecoles des Mines.)

74. He was the last king to govern France.

   A. Louis XVIII

   B. Louis-Philippe

   C. Napoléon III

   D. Charles X

B is correct: Louis Philippe was King between 1830 and 1848. Louis XVIII reigned between 1815 and 1824, and Charles X between 1824 and 1830. As for Napoléon III, he was an Emperor, not a King: his reign ended with the disastrous battle of Sedan against Prussia, in 1871.

75. Which provinces were lost to Germany after the Franco-Prussian war?

   A. Alsace and Lorraine

   B. Lorraine and Savoie

   C. Bourgogne and Champagne

   D. Alsace and Savoie

The answer is A: these two provinces are, although on the French side, are on the border that separates both countries.

76. This leader of the French army during WWII became president of the 5th Republic.

   A. Général Pétain

   B. Général de Gaulle

   C. Général Foch

   D. Général Joffe

B is correct. General de Gaulle was not only President, he gave France a new Constitution, which initiated the Vth Republic.

77. **In which province is Chamonix located?**

A. Provence

B. Savoie

C. Lorraine

D. Languedoc

B is right: Chamonix is a ski resort in the Alps, in the province of Savoie.

78. **In which province is Brest located?**

A. Languedoc

B. Bretagne

C. Normandie

D. Picardie

B is correct.

79. **Which mountains separate France from Switzerland.**

A. Les Alpes

B. Les Pyrénées

C. Le Jura

D. Les Vosges

C is the right answer.

80. **Which river is the longest in France, along which are many chateaux?**

A. La Seine

B. La Garonne

C. Le Rhone

D. La Loire

D is right.

81. **Which island was the retreat for the painter Gaugin?**

A. La Martinique

B. Tahiti

C. Haïti

D. La Guyane Française

B is the correct answer. The Polynesian influence is very obvious in the work he did while in Tahiti: the colour of the people's skin, in particular, is a beautiful golden brown.

82. **Which is the next most important person in the French government after the president?**

A. Le Maire de Paris

B. Le Premier Ministre

C. Le Consul General

D. Le Député de l'Assemblée Nationale

B is correct.

83. **How long does France's presidential term last?**

A. 7 ans

B. 5 ans

C. 4 ans

D. 3 ans

In 1958, De Gaulle became the first president of the Vth Republic for 7 years. Reelected in 1965. he resigned after losing a referendum over "regionalisations) in 1969. Pompidou succeeded him, but died of cancer in 1974. Then Giscard was elected after defeating a certain Mitterand. In 1981 (May 10), Mitterrand won a historic election that made the socialist party the first in the Hexagon. He completed two 7-year terms, but did not run in 1995. Chirac won the election for 7 years. However the constitution was changed to a 5-year term when his term expired. That's why the presidential election will be held in April of 2007. So only B is correct.

84. Which of the following allows you to do your banking and call your friends?

   A. La Banque Nationale de Paris

   B. Le Minitel

   C. Le TGV

   D. Le RER

B is right: the Minitel, introduced in the 1980's, is similar to a small computer, and allows you to get into the white or yellow pages of the phone book, to make or cancel a reservation, or to correspond with other people who are also using their Minitel.

85. Léopold Senghor, born African, raised in France, was the 1st president of this country.

   A. La Mauritanie

   B. L'Algérie

   C. Le Sénégal

   D. Le Liberia

C is right: Léopold Sédar Senghor's work features many of his country's beauty and mythology.

86. Which of the following is one of the most important exports of France?

   A. Le fromage.

   B. Le pétrole

   C. Le coton

   D. Le cacao

A is right. France boast for having more than 400 varieties of cheeses.

87. Which of the following was a famous French film director and also married to Candice Bergen?

   A. Francois Truffaut

   B. Alain Resnais

   C. Louis Malle

   D. Claude Lelouch

C is right.

88. **Which of the following is the current president of France (1995)?**

    A. Francois Mitterand

    B. Pierre Mauroy

    C. Jacques Chirac

    D. Michel Rocard

C is right. As explained, Chirac has served one 7-year term (1995-2002), and is completing a 5-year term ending in 2007.

89. **Which of the following singers is popular in the U.S., Canada, and France?**

    A. Céline Dion

    B. Brigitte Bardot

    C. Mireille Mathieu

    D. Chantal Goya

A is right: Brigitte Bardot (B) is an actress and she sang a few songs, but she is now in her seventies. Mireille Mathieu (C) is also well liked, but she does not have the huge public of Céline Dion. Chantal Goya (D) sings mainly for children.

90. **Which French author was voted the most popular among the French according to Le Figaro Magazine?**

    A. Victor Hugo

    B. Rabelais

    C. Corneille

    D. Molière

A is right: Victor Hugo has been an extremely popular poet ever since he was alive. When he died, a huge crowd followed his casket being carried down the streets of Paris. He is one of the few buried in the Panthéon in Paris.

91. **Which of the following past times are most similar in the U.S. and France?**

    A. Food

    B. Politics

    C. Sports

    D. Music

D is the right answer, even though A, B and C are also hugely popular.

92. **In which country do they celebrate the feast of Jean-Baptiste, le 24 juin?**

    A. Canada

    B. Martinique

    C. France

    D. Guadeloupe

A is the correct answer.

Literature

93. **Which is the 1st document written in old French?**

    A. Chanson de Roland

    B. Le Roman de Renard

    C. Les Miracles et Mysteres

    D. Les Serments de Strasbourg

D is the right answer.

94. **Who was the head of the group of 7 poets called the Pléiade?**

    A. François Villon

    B. Malherbe

    C. Charles d'Orléans

    D. Pierre de Ronsard

D is the correct answer. Du Bellay was another very important member of this group.

95. **Which of the following was the main literary movement of the 17th century?**

    A. Le Romantisme

    B. Le Classicisme

    C. Le Réalisme

    D. L'Impressionisme

B is correct. A , C and D are all movements of the XIXth Century.

96. **Which of the following wrote the famous "Maximes"?**

    A. Le duc de La Rochefoucauld

    B. Mme de Sévigné

    C. La Bruyère

    D. René Descartes

A is the right answer.

97. **Who is famous for the following quote?**

    "Je pense, donc je suis."

    A. Montesquieu

    B. Descartes

    C. Voltaire

    D. Pascal

The answer is B: Descarts.

98. **Which is the name for the literary style, began in the salons, with emphasis on preciseness of words.**

    A. La préciosité

    B. La clarté

    C. La satire

    D. L'ordre

A is right: this is a movement of the XVIIth century, which Molière makes fun of in L'Ecole des Femmes, Les Femmes savantes and Les Précieuses ridicules. This movement was excessively refined and artificial: Mlle de Scudéry, Madame de Lafayette and Honoré d'Urfé are the main writers of this group of writers.

99. **Which of the following wrote Le Rouge et le Noir - a psychological novel?**

    A. Alphonse de Lamartine

    B. Honoré de Balzac

    C. Stendhal

    D. Châteaubriand

The answer is C.

100. **In which of the following stories does Gustave Flaubert give us a picture of life in a small Normandy town?**

    A. La Parure

    B. Eugénie Grandet

    C. Madame Bovary

    D. René

C is the right answer: La Parure is by Maupassant, Eugénie Grandet by Balzac, and René by Châteaubriand.

101. **Which of the following exemplifies the sentiment of 19th century literature?**

    A. La vérité

    B. Le malaise

    C. La tradition classique

    D. La discipline

B is right. Châteaubriand was one of the first to express this sentiment in René and Atala.

102. **Which of the following was the head of the existentialist movement?**

    A. Anatole France

    B. Jean Paul Sartre

    C. Albert Camus

    D. Antoine de St. Exupery

B is the right answer. Anatole France was a XIXth century writer. Albert Camus was an Existentialist, but his brand of Existentialism was different from that of Sartre. As for St Exupéry, he was not an Existentialist.

103. **Which of the following wrote La Peste and La Chute?**

    A. Anatole France

    B. Jean-Paul Sartre

    C. Camus

    D. Jean Anouilh

C is correct.

104. **Which cartoon is no longer published in French newspapers?**

    A. Tintin

    B. Peanuts

    C. Family Circus

    D. Astérix

D is right.

105. **In the French song, Sur le Pont d'Avignon, what are the men and ladies doing?**

    A. ils dansent

    B. ils chantent

    C. ils regardent les bateaux

    D. ils racontent des histoires

A is the correct answer.

106. **Which of the following sculpted le Penseur?**

    A. Picasso

    B. Rodin

    C. Aristide Maillol

    D. Jean-Antoine Houdon

B is correct: Le Penseur is Rodin's most famous sculpture.

107. **Which of the following composed Au clair de la Lune?**

    A. Bizet

    B. Debussy

    C. Ravel

    D. Saint Saëns

B is correct.

108. **Which of the following is known for his painting of dancers at the Opera?**

    A. Renoir

    B. Manet

    C. Cézanne

    D. Degas

D is the right answer.

109. **Which of the following began the style of pointillisme?**

    A. Claude Monet

    B. Edouard Manet

    C. Georges Seurat

    D. Auguste Renoir

C is the correct answer: it becomes obvious when one looks at his paintings.

Pedagogy

110. **Which of the following activities will help the students most easily <u>in remembering</u> the placement of direct/indirect objects?**

    A. Singing - Au Clair de la Lune

    B. Writing activities

    C. Partner practice

    D. Listening to a story

A is correct.

111. **What is a fun way to assess knowledge of verb structures?**

    A. Conjugating verbs

    B. Writing activities

    C. Play 20 questions

    D. Play dice-verb game with partner

D is both a fun and effective way to get to know verb structures.

113. **What is an easy way to help build reading comprehension and vocabulary retention at the first level?**

    A. Cognate instruction

    B. Flash cards

    C. Partner practice

    D. Translation

A is the right answer: cognates help learn vocabulary immensely.

114. **Which of the following would best test a student's reading comprehension in French III?**

    A. Ask student questions

    B. Have student translate selection

    C. Have student make up questions

    D. Have student write a resume of the selection

D is correct.

114. **Which method would best teach students the art of letter writing?**

    A. Translating sentences

    B. French pen pals

    C. Write notes in French to friends in class

    D. Copy example letters from the text

B is the right answer: having an ongoing correspondence with a pen pal will help a lot.

115. Which method will allow assessment of students of written skills already learned?

A. Guided composition

B. Translation sentences

C. Write a resume of story

D. Writing exercises

A is correct. The help brought about by writing compositions cannot be over emphasized.

116. Select the activity best suited to practice speaking skills.

A. Partner practice

B. Repeat after the teacher

C. Read aloud

D. Listen to tape then record separately the same words selection.

D is the right answer: recording sentences after listening to a tape helps the student compare his/her skills to the way the words are pronounced on the tape.

117. Which method is best for teaching listening skills?

A. Listening to French cassettes

B. Partner practice

C. Constant use of French by teacher in classroom

D. Giving dictations to students

C is correct: the teacher should speak French in the classroom as much as possible, right from the first level, provided he or she masters that difficult skill.

118. Which game would be fun to practice listening skills?

A. Pictionary

B. Jeopardy in French

C. Partner practice

D. 20 Questions

D is the right answer: in order to play 20 Questions, the student has to listen very carefully to the French sentences, and has to come up with grammatically correct answers.

119. **Select the activity best suited to learning culture.**

    A. Global bingo

    B. Show and tell

    C. Read book

    D. Show a movie

B is correct.

120. **Which would not be appropriate for teaching and explaining culture?**

    A. Show and tell

    B. Pictionary

    C. Movie

    D. Global Bingo

B would not be helpful, since Pictionary relies on drawing instead of speaking.

XAMonline, INC. 21 Orient Ave. Melrose, MA 02176

Toll Free number 800-509-4128

TO ORDER Fax 781-662-9268 OR www.XAMonline.com
<u>PRAXIS SERIES</u>   - PRAXIS - 2009

Address:

City, State Zip

Credit card number_____-_____-_____-_____   expiration_____

EMAIL _____

PHONE   **FAX**

13# ISBN 2009	TITLE	Qty	Retail	Total
978-1-60787-043-2	Art Sample Test 10133			
978-1-60787-031-9	Biology 20231, 20232, 20235			
978-1-58197-691-5	Chemistry 20241 20242, 20245			
978-1-60787-046-3	Earth and Space Sciences 20571			
978-1-60787-033-3	Special Education: Knowledge-Based Core Principles 20351			
978-1-60787-037-1	Special Education: Teaching Students with Behavioral Disorders/Emotional Disturbance 0371			
978-1-60787-035-7	PRAXIS Early Childhood 020, 022			
978-1-60787-041-8	Educational Leadership 0410			
978-1-60787-048-7	Elementary Education 0011, 0012, 0014, 0016			
978-1-60787-044-9	English Language, Literature, and Composition 10041			
978-1-60787-053-1	French Sample Test 0173			
978-1-60787-042-5	Fundamental Subjects 0511			
978-1-60787-032-6	School Guidance & Counseling 20420			
978-1-58197-268-9	General Science 10435			
978-1-60787-039-5	Library Media Specialist 0310			
978-1-60787-049-4	Mathematics 10061, 20063			
978-1-58197-269-6	Middle School English Language Arts 10049			
978-1-58197-343-3	Middle School Mathematics 20069			
978-1-58197-263-4	Middle School Social Studies 0089			
978-1-60787-040-1	Physical Education 10091			
978-1-60787-047-0	Physics 0265			
978-1-60787-038-8	ParaPro Assessment 0755			
978-1-60787-036-4	PPST I: Basic Skills 0710, 0720, 0730			
978-1-58197-054-8	Government/Poltical Science 10930			
978-1-58197-577-2	Principals of Learning and Teaching 30521, 30522, 30523,			
978-1-60787-034-0	Reading 0200, 0201, 0202			
978-1-58197-696-0	Social Studies 10081			
978-1-58197-718-9	Spanish 10191, 30194			
978-1-60787-057-9	353 Exceptional Student Core Content Knowledge (New)			
978-1-60787-055-5	382 Education of Exceptional Students - Learning Disability			
978-1-60787-056-2	542 Ed Students Disabilities Mild to Moderate disabilities			
	Shipping $8.70 1 book, $11.00 2 books, $15.00 3			
	TOTAL			

CPSIA information can be obtained at www.ICGtesting.com
Printed in the USA
BVOW051459081011

273150BV00001B/1/P